the complete drumset rudiments

by Peter Magadini

Edited by Rick Mattingly

ISBN 978-0-7935-8372-0

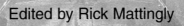

HAL•LEONARD® CORPORATION

7777 W. BLUEMOUND RD. P.O. BOX 13819 MILWAUKEE, WI 53213

Visit Hal Leonard Online at
www.halleonard.com

about the author

Peter Magadini is a professional drummer and percussionist who has performed with many internationally recognized artists and organizations including The George Duke Trio, Diana Ross, Don Menza, Sonny Stitt and Mose Allison, to name a few. As a percussionist Peter has played with the Berkshire Music Festival Orchestra at Tanglewood, the Toronto Symphony Orchestra and the Fromm Festival of Contemporary Music.

Magadini has four recordings released under his own name, including *Night Dreamers* (The Pete Magadini Quintet), *Live at Claudios* (with Don Menza) and *Polyrhythm* (with George Duke). Peter has authored such books as the award-winning *Polyrhythms the Musician's Guide* (ranked number six in *Modern Drummer* magazine's survey of "The 25 Greatest Drum Books"), *Learn to Play the Drumset* Vols. I and II and *Polyrhythms for the Drumset*. Many of the world's leading drummers and percussionists have studied from and endorse Magadini's books and materials, including a select number that Peter has had the opportunity to teach personally.

Peter holds two degrees in Percussion and Performance from the San Francisco Conservatory of Music and the University of Toronto. His teachers have included Don Bothwell, Roy Burns, Roland Kohloff (solo timpanist, New York Philharmonic) and North Indian tabla master Mahapurush Misra.

Peter Magadini endorses Yamaha Drums, Aquarian drumheads, Calato/Regal Tip drumsticks, and Paiste cymbals.

the complete drumset rudiments

contents

CD tracks

1 Solo from the recording *Drum Dreams*
performed by Peter Magadini

2 Introduction to Rudiments

3 Select 28 Snare Drum Rudiments

4 "Fantasy for Drums" excerpt
performed by Niko Magadini

5 The 26 Drumset Rudiments

6 "The Modulator" solo from the album *Polyrhythm*
performed by Peter Magadini

7 *Agbekor* African ensemble rhythm "Welcome From the Hunt"
performed by Peter Magadini

8 The 26 Polyrhythm Rudiments

9 "Katmandu" solo from the recording *Pete Magadini on Drums, Then To Now*
performed by Peter Magadini

Foreword

The rudiments are often called the "building blocks of drumming." The first set of standardized American drum rudiments was created by the National Association of Rudimental Drummers (N.A.R.D.) in the 1930s, and consisted of 26 rudiments that were considered essential by the N.A.R.D. members. In 1984 the Percussive Arts Society (PAS) expanded the list by compiling a set of 40 International Drum Rudiments, which contained the original 26 N.A.R.D. rudiments as well as drum corps, European, orchestral and contemporary snare drum rudiments that had become popular. (The PAS International Drum Rudiments are shown on pages 22 and 23.)

Many drumset players have used the rudiments for hand and technique development, as well as to create rhythmic patterns that can be applied to a wide variety of musical styles. You can hear a rudimental influence in the work of jazz drummer Joe Morello (who wrote an influential book called *Rudimental Jazz*) and in many of the drum parts created by Steve Gadd.

As with any musical lick or technique, mastery of the rudiments is not an end in itself, but rather a means to an end. In a column written for *International Musician* in the 1950s, *Stick Control* author George Lawrence Stone replied to a letter from a reader who said, "A brother drummer claims that there are only two rudiments in drumming, the single stroke and the double stroke, and that these are all you have to know." Stone replied, "Tell the brother that there are only 26 letters in the alphabet, and that's all *he* has to know, until he finds out they have to be strung together in some sort of way before they make sense."

— Rick Mattingly

Pete Magadini's Select 28 Snare Drum Rudiments

The snare drum rudiments selected for this book were chosen primarily from the 40 PAS International Drum Rudiments, except for the Three-stroke Ruff with alternating sticking. These 28 "select" snare drum rudiments were used as the basis of the 26 Drumset Rudiments and the 26 Polyrhythm Rudiments. (Note that the Six-stroke and Ten-stroke rolls appear only in the Drumset Rudiments and the Three-stroke Ruff only appears in the Polyrhythm Rudiments.)

How to practice the material in this book

It is suggested that you master the 28 Select Snare Drum Rudiments first, before going on to the Drumset Rudiments and Polyrhythm Rudiments. The results of working with this rudimental study will be apparent in *all* of your playing skills.

As you develop your hand technique with the Snare Drum Rudiments, your hand and foot technique with the Drumset Rudiments, and your polyrhythmic technique with the Polyrhythm Rudiments, use your imagination to incorporate these rudiments into new patterns that you can apply to the drumset. Adopt them into your own drumming vocabulary in order to achieve creative expression based on ideas you come up with while practicing.

Good luck!

— Peter Magadini

The Recording

The compact disc that accompanies this book contains demonstrations of The Select 28 Snare Drum Rudiments, The 26 Drumset Rudiments and The 26 Polyrhythm Rudiments, performed by Peter Magadini. In addition, the CD includes five short solos that act as preludes to the rudimental segments, and that demonstrate actual applications of rudimental ideas into musical situations. Notation for three of the solos can be found within the book, so that you can study the patterns and hear how they sound. The first and last solos are meant to entertain and inspire.

Notation key

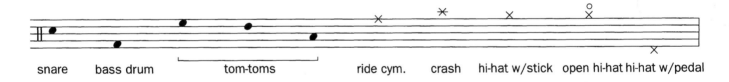

snare   bass drum   tom-toms   ride cym.   crash   hi-hat w/stick open hi-hat hi-hat w/pedal

The Select 28 Snare Drum Rudiments

Note: With roll rudiments, the first measure shows how the roll is played and the second measure shows how it is typically notated.

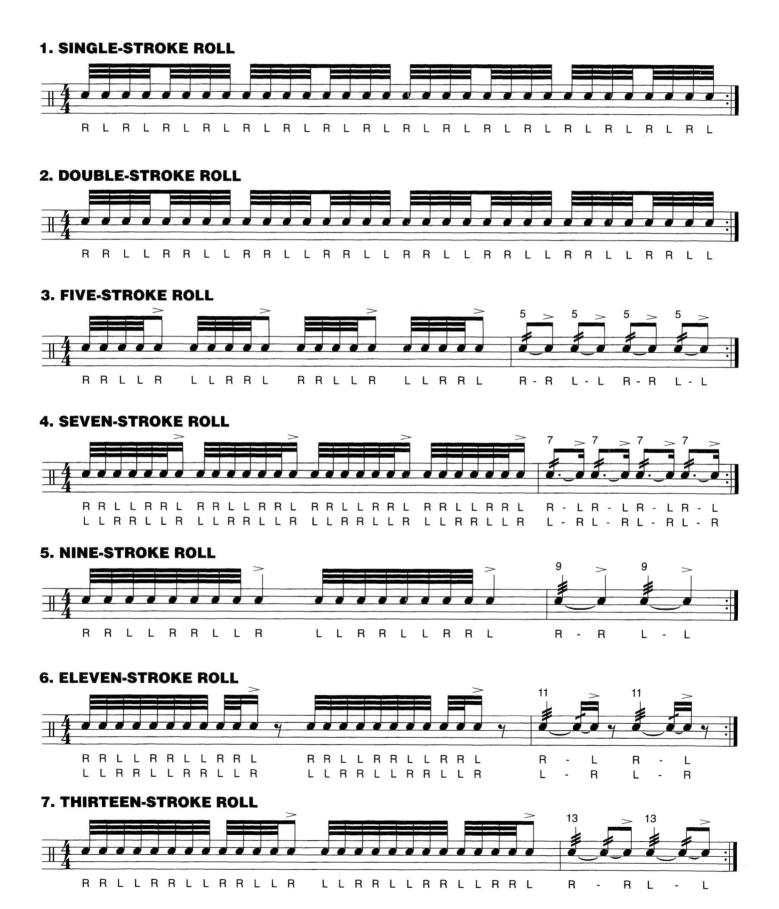

1. SINGLE-STROKE ROLL

R L R L R L R L R L R L R L R L R L R L R L R L R L R L R L R L

2. DOUBLE-STROKE ROLL

R R L L R R L L R R L L R R L L R R L L R R L L R R L L R R L L

3. FIVE-STROKE ROLL

R R L L R   L L R R L   R R L L R   L L R R L   R - R L - L R - R L - L

4. SEVEN-STROKE ROLL

R R L L R R L   R R L L R R L   R R L L R R L   R R L L R R L   R - L R - L R - L R - L
L L R R L L R   L L R R L L R   L L R R L L R   L L R R L L R   L - R L - R L - R L - R

5. NINE-STROKE ROLL

R R L L R R L L R   L L R R L L R R L   R - R L - L

6. ELEVEN-STROKE ROLL

R R L L R R L L R R L   R R L L R R L L R R L   R - L   R - L
L L R R L L R R L L R   L L R R L L R R L L R   L - R   L - R

7. THIRTEEN-STROKE ROLL

R R L L R R L L R R L L R   L L R R L L R R L L R R L   R - R L - L

6

8. FLAM

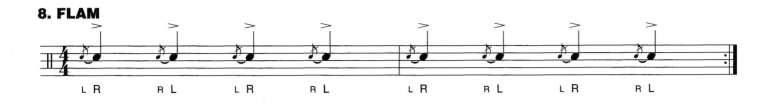

9. FLAM TAP

10. FLAMACUE

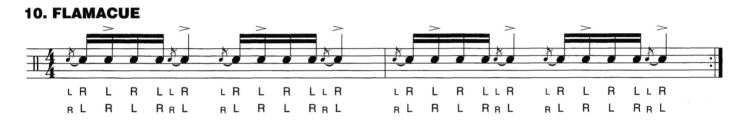

11. FLAM ACCENT

FLAM PARADIDDLE

13. SWISS ARMY TRIPLET

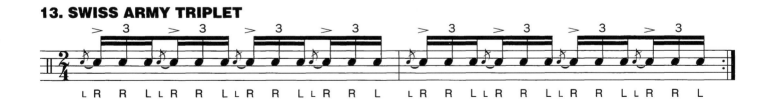

14. FLAM PARADIDDLE-DIDDLE

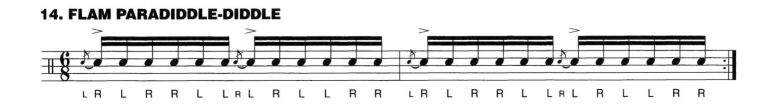

15. DRAG

LLR　RRL　LLR　RRL　LLR　RRL　LLR　RRL

16. SINGLE DRAG

R　LLR　L　RRL　R　LLR　L　RRL　R　LLR　L　RRL　R　LLR　L　RRL

17. DOUBLE DRAG

LLR　LLR　L　RRL　RRL　R　LLR　LLR　L　RRL　RRL　R

18. PARADIDDLE

R L R R L R L L R L R R L R L L　R L R R L R L L R L R R L R L L

19. DOUBLE PARADIDDLE

R L R L R R L R L R L L　R L R L R R L R L R L L

20. TRIPLE PARADIDDLE

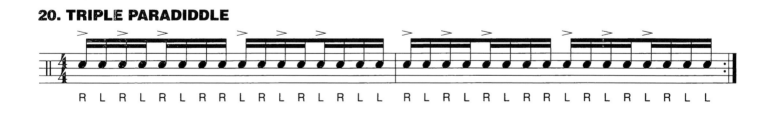

R L R L R L R R L R L R L R L L　R L R L R L R R L R L R L R L L

21. SINGLE RATAMACUE

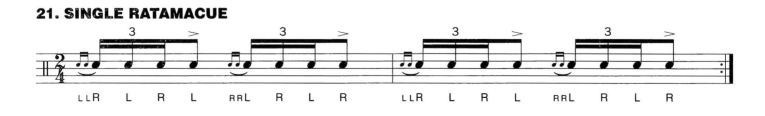

LLR　L　R　L　RRL　R　L　R　LLR　L　R　L　RRL　R　L　R

8

22. DOUBLE RATAMACUE

LLR   LLR   L R L   RRL   RRL   R L R   LLR   LLR   L R L   RRL   RRL   R L R

23. TRIPLE RATAMACUE

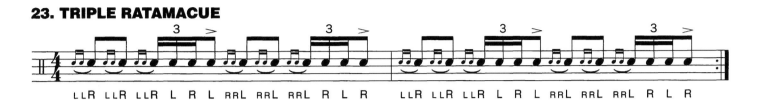

LLR LLR LLR L R L RRL RRL RRL R L R   LLR LLR LLR L R L RRL RRL RRL R L R

24. LESSON 25

LLR L R LLR L R LLR L R LLR L R   LLR L R LLR L R LLR L R LLR L R
RRL R L RRL R L RRL R L RRL R L   RRL R L RRL R L RRL R L RRL R L

25. THREE-STROKE RUFF

RLR   LRL   RLR   LRL   RLR   LRL   RLR   LRL

26. FOUR-STROKE RUFF

LRLR   RLRL   LRLR   RLRL   LRLR   RLRL   LRLR   RLRL

27. SIX-STROKE ROLL

RLLRRLRLLRRLRLLRRLRLLRRL   RLLRRLRLLRRLRLLRRLRLLRRL
LRRLLRLRRLLRLRRLLRLRRLLR   LRRLLRLRRLLRLRRLLRLRRLLR

28. TEN-STROKE ROLL

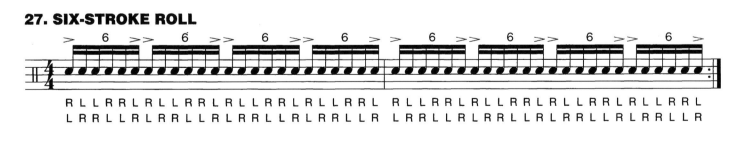

RRLLRRLLR L   RRLLRRLLR L   R - R L   R - R L
LLRRLLRRL R   LLRRLLRRL R   L - L R   L - L R

9

Commissioned for the 1991
Percussive Arts Society International Convention
Fantasy for Drums
(excerpt)

Rod Lincoln

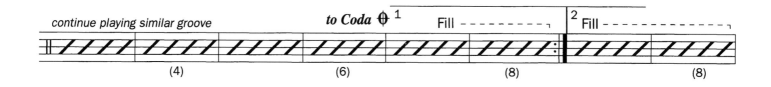

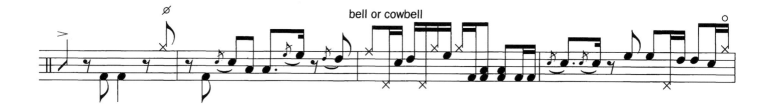

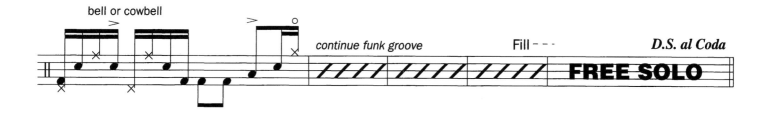

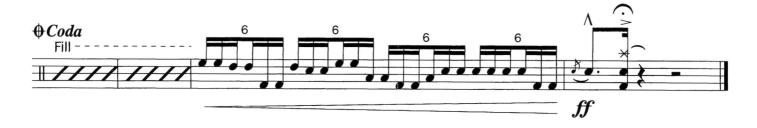

The 26 Drumset Rudiments

Note: If you have a double bass drum setup or are using a double bass drum pedal, leave the hi-hat part out and alternate the bass drum part between both feet. The only exception is rudiment 13, the Flam Accent, in which the second bass drum will play the notated hi-hat part.

1. SINGLE-STROKE ROLL

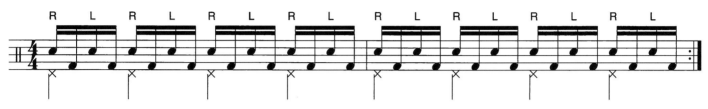

2. DOUBLE-STROKE ROLL

3. FIVE-STROKE ROLL

4. SIX-STROKE ROLL

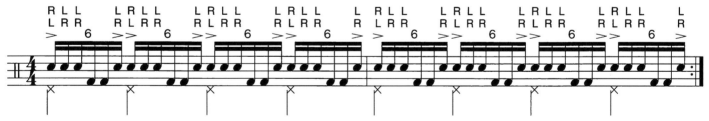

5. SEVEN-STROKE ROLL

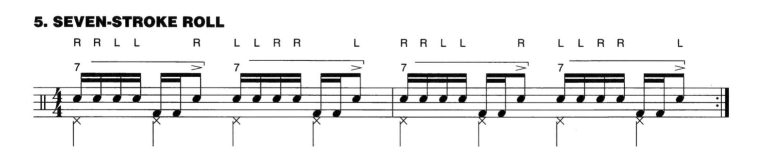

6. NINE-STROKE ROLL

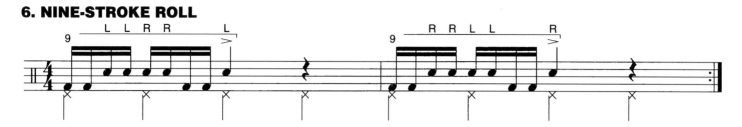

7. TEN-STROKE ROLL

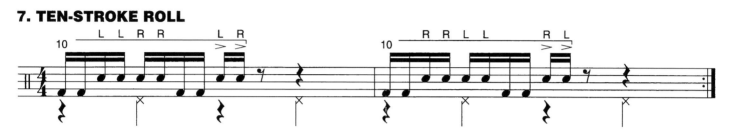

8. ELEVEN-STROKE ROLL

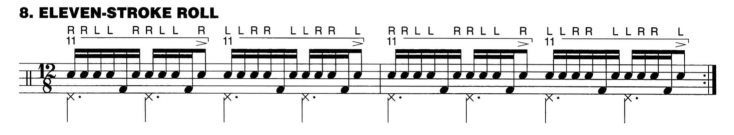

9. THIRTEEN-STROKE ROLL

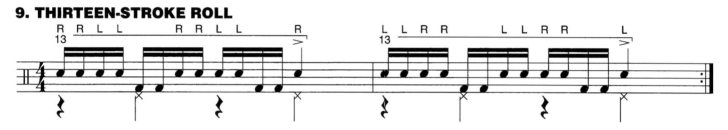

10. FLAM

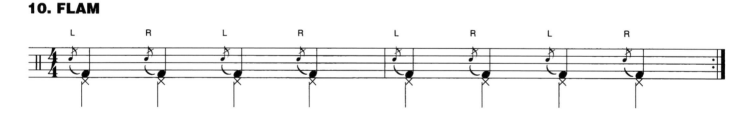

11. FLAM TAP

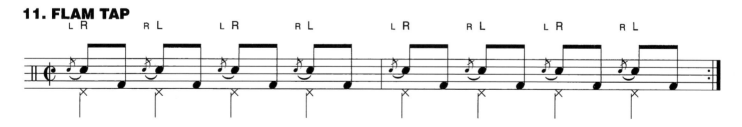

12. FLAMACUE

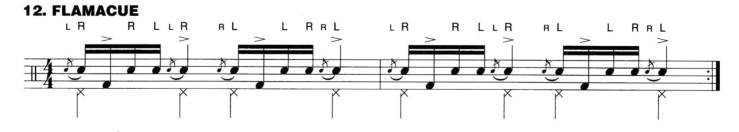

13. FLAM ACCENT

14. FLAM PARADIDDLE

15. SWISS TRIPLET

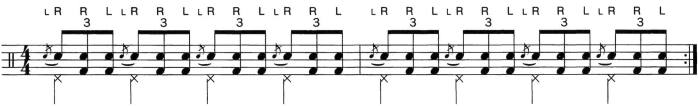

16. FLAM PARADIDDLE-DIDDLE

17. DRAG (FLAM)

18. SINGLE DRAG (FLAM)

19. DOUBLE DRAG (FLAM)

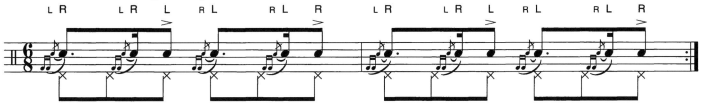

20. SINGLE PARADIDDLE

21. DOUBLE PARADIDDLE

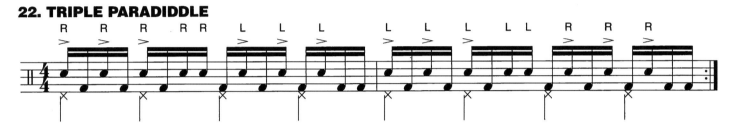

22. TRIPLE PARADIDDLE

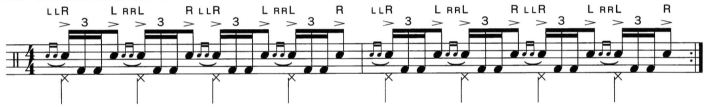

23. SINGLE RATAMACUE

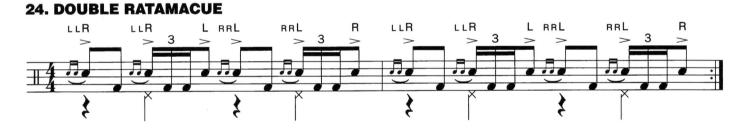

24. DOUBLE RATAMACUE

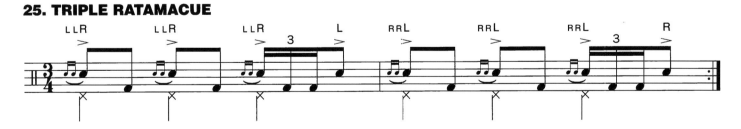

25. TRIPLE RATAMACUE

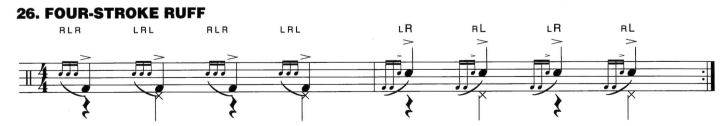

26. FOUR-STROKE RUFF

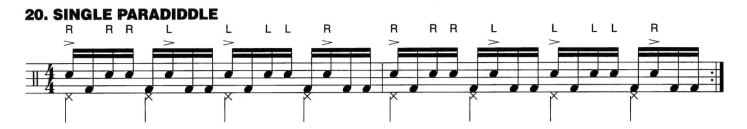

The Modulator

From the album *Polyrhythm*

R L L R L L R L L

Agbekor

African rhythms have been an intriguing mystery to me ever since I began to play drums. During a drum seminar at Concordia University, my students and I listened to and analyzed the Ewe ensemble called *Agbekor* – a dance performed by women welcoming men home from battle. Within the ensemble parts you can find all the essential elements of jazz, Afro-Cuban and Brazilian rhythms.

The ensemble is so rich in rhythmic expression and suggestive counter-rhythms that I created a drumset variation based on the ensemble arrangement, which is notated below. This is only one possible arrangement of the *Agbekor* rhythms into a drumset part. I encourage drummers to create their own arrangements.

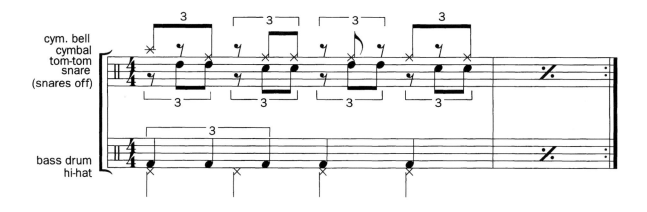

The 26 Polyrhythm Rudiments

Learn the basic polyrhythm of each rudiment over the underlying pulse before applying the actual rudiment. Play rudiments 1 and 2, the single-stroke and double-stroke rolls, by gradually increasing and then decreasing the speed while maintaining a steady ostinato pattern on the bass drum and hi-hat, as in the four examples below. If not using a drumset, pat your foot in an even, steady pulse. For the remainder of the Polyrhythm Rudiments, play the bass drum, tap your foot, or use a click track or metronome to maintain the basic pulse.

Bass drum and hi-hat ostinatos

5. NINE-STROKE ROLL

6. ELEVEN-STROKE ROLL

7. THIRTEEN-STROKE ROLL

8. FLAM

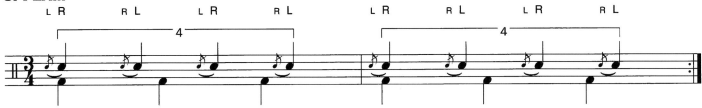

9. FLAM TAP

10. FLAMACUE

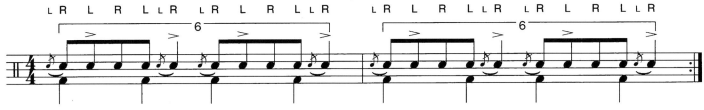

11. FLAM ACCENT

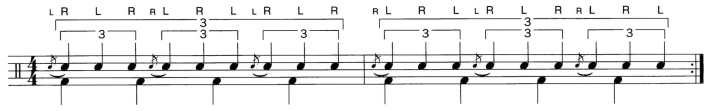

12. FLAM PARADIDDLE

13. SWISS ARMY TRIPLET

14. FLAM PARADIDDLE-DIDDLE

15. DRAG

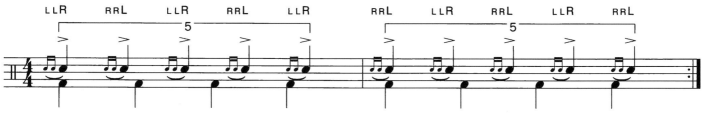

16. SINGLE DRAG

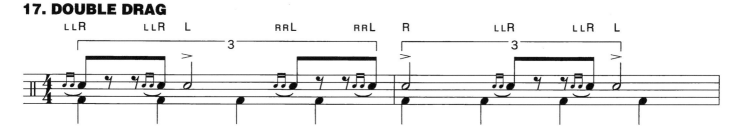

17. DOUBLE DRAG

18. PARADIDDLE

Polyrhythm Pyramid

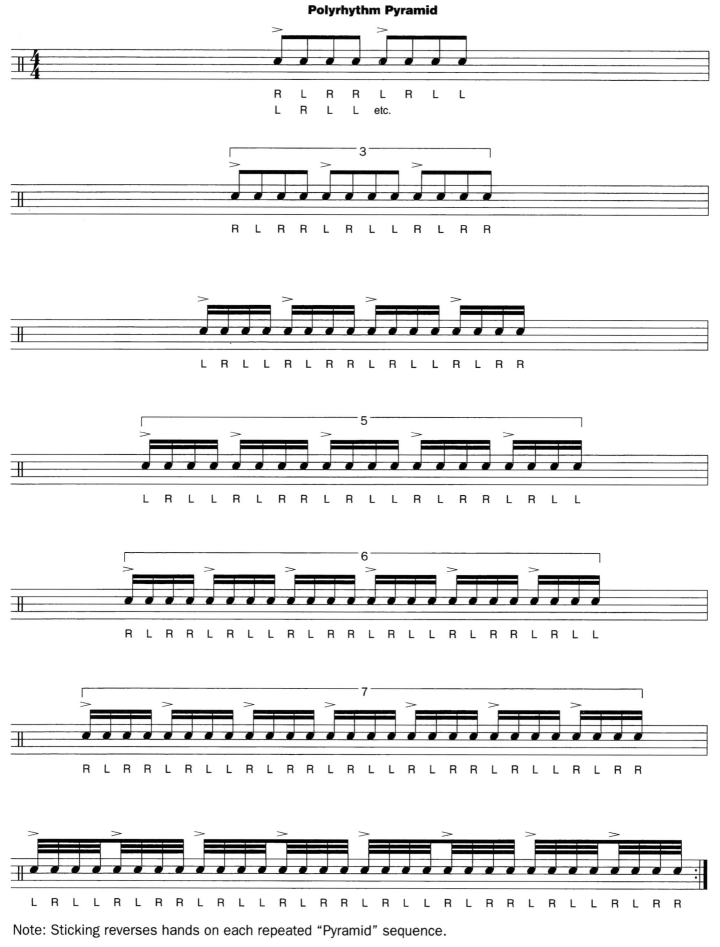

Note: Sticking reverses hands on each repeated "Pyramid" sequence.

19. DOUBLE PARADIDDLE

20. TRIPLE PARADIDDLE

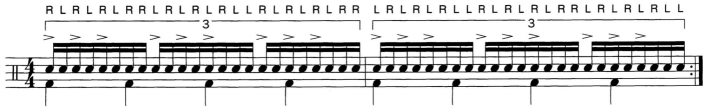

21. SINGLE RATAMACUE

22. DOUBLE RATAMACUE

23. TRIPLE RATAMACUE

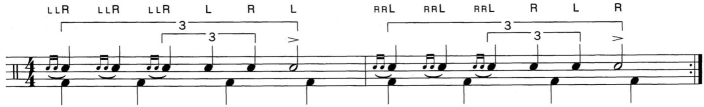

24. LESSON 25

25 & 26. THREE- AND FOUR-STROKE RUFFS

PERCUSSIVE ARTS SOCIETY INTERNATIONAL DRUM RUDIMENTS

All rudiments should be practiced: *open* (slow) to *close* (fast) to *open* (slow) and/or at an even moderate march tempo.

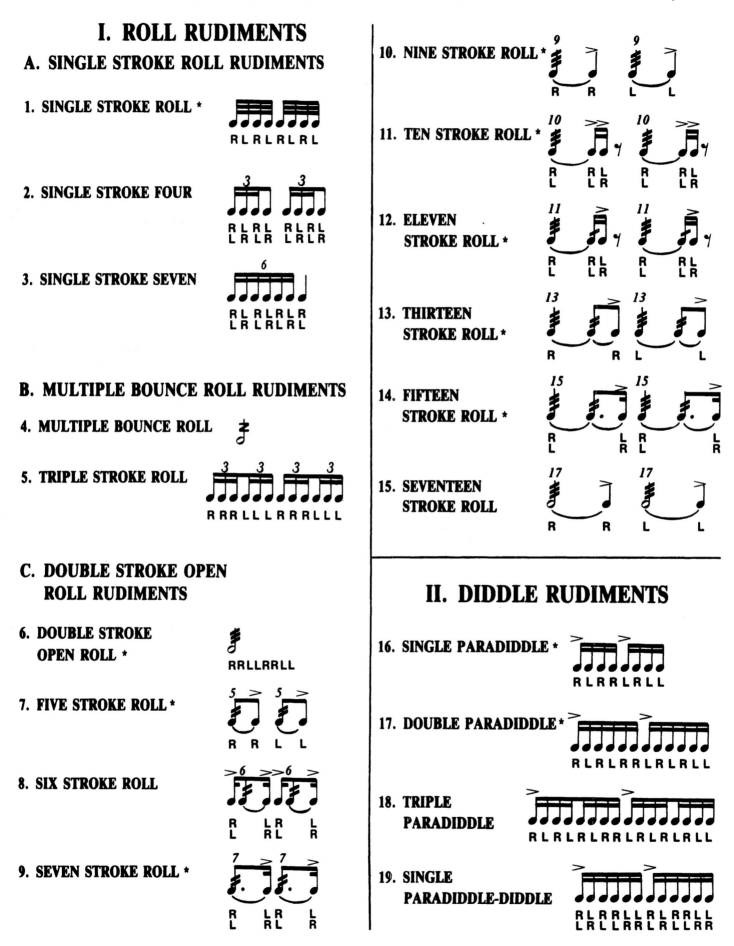

I. ROLL RUDIMENTS

A. SINGLE STROKE ROLL RUDIMENTS

1. SINGLE STROKE ROLL *

2. SINGLE STROKE FOUR

3. SINGLE STROKE SEVEN

B. MULTIPLE BOUNCE ROLL RUDIMENTS

4. MULTIPLE BOUNCE ROLL

5. TRIPLE STROKE ROLL

C. DOUBLE STROKE OPEN ROLL RUDIMENTS

6. DOUBLE STROKE OPEN ROLL *

7. FIVE STROKE ROLL *

8. SIX STROKE ROLL

9. SEVEN STROKE ROLL *

10. NINE STROKE ROLL *

11. TEN STROKE ROLL *

12. ELEVEN STROKE ROLL *

13. THIRTEEN STROKE ROLL *

14. FIFTEEN STROKE ROLL *

15. SEVENTEEN STROKE ROLL

II. DIDDLE RUDIMENTS

16. SINGLE PARADIDDLE *

17. DOUBLE PARADIDDLE *

18. TRIPLE PARADIDDLE

19. SINGLE PARADIDDLE-DIDDLE

*These rudiments are also included in the original Standard 26 American Drum Rudiments.

III. FLAM RUDIMENTS

IV. DRAG RUDIMENTS

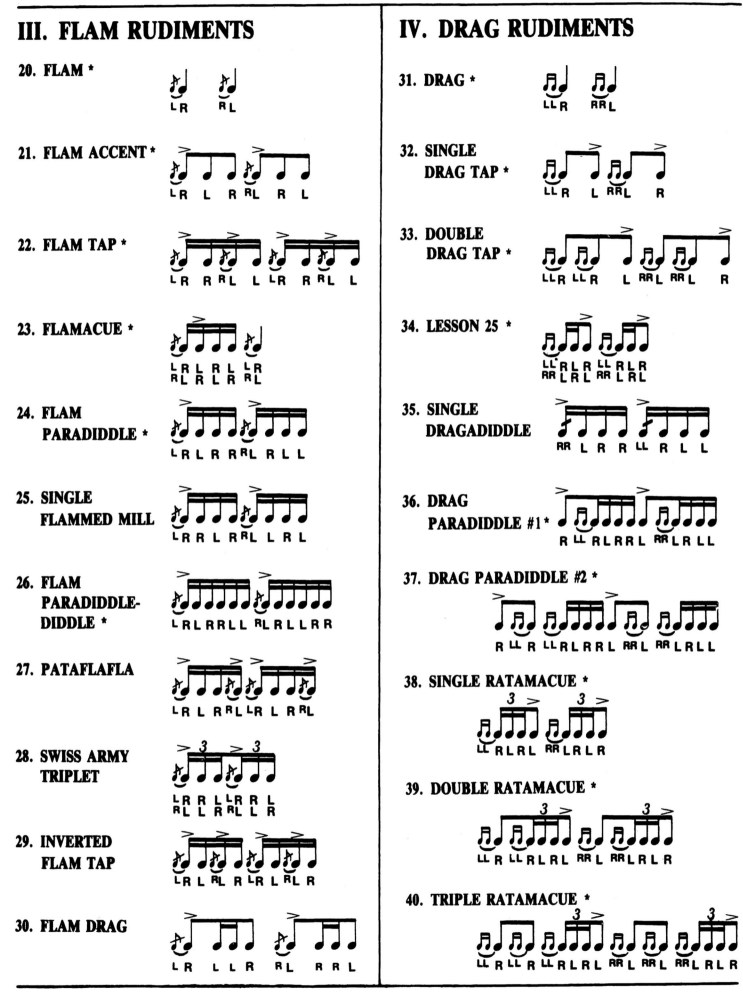

20. FLAM *

21. FLAM ACCENT *

22. FLAM TAP *

23. FLAMACUE *

24. FLAM PARADIDDLE *

25. SINGLE FLAMMED MILL

26. FLAM PARADIDDLE-DIDDLE *

27. PATAFLAFLA

28. SWISS ARMY TRIPLET

29. INVERTED FLAM TAP

30. FLAM DRAG

31. DRAG *

32. SINGLE DRAG TAP *

33. DOUBLE DRAG TAP *

34. LESSON 25 *

35. SINGLE DRAGADIDDLE

36. DRAG PARADIDDLE #1 *

37. DRAG PARADIDDLE #2 *

38. SINGLE RATAMACUE *

39. DOUBLE RATAMACUE *

40. TRIPLE RATAMACUE *

YOU CAN'T BEAT OUR DRUM BOOKS!

Bass Drum Control
Best Seller for More Than 50 Years!
by Colin Bailey
This perennial favorite among drummers helps players develop their bass drum technique and increase their flexibility through the mastery of exercises.
06620020 Book/Online Audio $17.99

The Complete Drumset Rudiments
by Peter Magadini
Use your imagination to incorporate these rudimental etudes into new patterns that you can apply to the drumset or tom toms as you develop your hand technique with the Snare Drum Rudiments, your hand and foot technique with the Drumset Rudiments and your polyrhythmic technique with the Polyrhythm Rudiments. Adopt them all into your own creative expressions based on ideas you come up with while practicing.
06620016 Book/CD Pack $14.95

Drum Aerobics
by Andy Ziker
A 52-week, one-exercise-per-day workout program for developing, improving, and maintaining drum technique. Players of all levels – beginners to advanced – will increase their speed, coordination, dexterity and accuracy. The online audio contains all 365 workout licks, plus play-along grooves in styles including rock, blues, jazz, heavy metal, reggae, funk, calypso, bossa nova, march, mambo, New Orleans 2nd Line, and lots more!
06620137 Book/Online Audio $19.99

Drumming the Easy Way!
The Beginner's Guide to Playing Drums for Students and Teachers
by Tom Hapke
Cherry Lane Music
Now with online audio! This book takes the beginning drummer through the paces – from reading simple exercises to playing great grooves and fills. Each lesson includes a preparatory exercise and a solo. Concepts and rhythms are introduced one at a time, so growth is natural and easy. Features large, clear musical print, intensive treatment of each individual drum figure, solos following each exercise to motivate students, and more!
02500876 Book/Online Audio..$19.99
02500191 Book...$14.99

The Drumset Musician – 2nd Edition
by Rod Morgenstein and Rick Mattingly
Containing hundreds of practical, usable beats and fills, *The Drumset Musician* teaches you how to apply a variety of patterns and grooves to the actual performance of songs. The accompanying online audio includes demos as well as 18 play-along tracks covering a wide range of rock, blues and pop styles, with detailed instructions on how to create exciting, solid drum parts.
00268369 Book/Online Audio...$19.99

Instant Guide to Drum Grooves
The Essential Reference for the Working Drummer
by Maria Martinez
Become a more versatile drumset player! From traditional Dixieland to cutting-edge hip-hop, *Instant Guide to Drum Grooves* is a handy source featuring 100 patterns that will prepare working drummers for the stylistic variety of modern gigs. The book includes essential beats and grooves in such styles as: jazz, shuffle, country, rock, funk, New Orleans, reggae, calypso, Brazilian and Latin.
06620056 Book/CD Pack $12.99

1001 Drum Grooves
The Complete Resource for Every Drummer
by Steve Mansfield
Cherry Lane Music
This book presents 1,001 drumset beats played in a variety of musical styles, past and present. It's ideal for beginners seeking a well-organized, easy-to-follow encyclopedia of drum grooves, as well as consummate professionals who want to bring their knowledge of various drum styles to new heights. Author Steve Mansfield presents: rock and funk grooves, blues and jazz grooves, ethnic grooves, Afro-Cuban and Caribbean grooves, and much more.
02500337 Book...$14.99

Polyrhythms – The Musician's Guide
by Peter Magadini
edited by Wanda Sykes
Peter Magadini's *Polyrhythms* is acclaimed the world over and has been hailed by *Modern Drummer* magazine as "by far the best book on the subject." Written for instrumentalists and vocalists alike, this book with online audio contains excellent solos and exercises that feature polyrhythmic concepts. Topics covered include: 6 over 4, 5 over 4, 7 over 4, 3 over 4, 11 over 4, and other rhythmic ratios; combining various polyrhythms; polyrhythmic time signatures; and much more. The audio includes demos of the exercises and is accessed online using the unique code in each book.
06620053 Book/Online Audio..$19.99

Joe Porcaro's Drumset Method – Groovin' with Rudiments
Patterns Applied to Rock, Jazz & Latin Drumset
by Joe Porcaro
Master teacher Joe Porcaro presents rudiments at the drumset in this sensational new edition of *Groovin' with Rudiments*. This book is chock full of exciting drum grooves, sticking patterns, fills, polyrhythmic adaptations, odd meters, and fantastic solo ideas in jazz, rock, and Latin feels. The online audio features 99 audio clip examples in many styles to round out this true collection of superb drumming material for every serious drumset performer.
06620129 Book/Online Audio $24.99

66 Drum Solos for the Modern Drummer
Rock • Funk • Blues • Fusion • Jazz
by Tom Hapke
Cherry Lane Music
66 Drum Solos for the Modern Drummer presents drum solos in all styles of music in an easy-to-read format. These solos are designed to help improve your technique, independence, improvisational skills, and reading ability on the drums and at the same time provide you with some cool licks that you can use right away in your own playing.
02500319 Book/Online Audio...$17.99

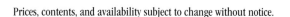

HAL•LEONARD®
www.halleonard.com